WHY SHOULD I SAVE ENERGY?

BARRON'S

Books in the
WHY SHOULD I? Series:

WHY SHOULD I Protect Nature?
WHY SHOULD I Recycle?
WHY SHOULD I Save Energy?
WHY SHOULD I Save Water?

First edition for the United States and Canada published in 2005
by Barron's Educational Series, Inc.

Published in Great Britain in 2001 by Hodder Wayland, an imprint
of Hodder Children's Books
© Copyright 2001 Hodder Wayland

All inquiries should be addressed to:
Barron's Educational Series, Inc.
250 Wireless Boulevard
Hauppauge, New York 11788
www.barronseduc.com

ISBN-13: 978 0-7641-3156-1   ISBN-10:0-7641-3156-7

Library of Congress Catalog Card No. 2004109999

Printed in China
9 8 7 6 5 4 3

WHY SHOULD I SAVE ENERGY?

Written by Jen Green

Illustrated by Mike Gordon

BARRON'S

In my family, we're careful about how we use energy.

We never used to be careful – we wasted lots of energy. We used the car all the time.

We always left the lights on,

we turned the heat
on full blast,

and we all took
hot baths with the
water nearly up
to the top.

Mmmmmm!

7

One evening my friend, Robert, was playing at our house.

I thought electricity was always right there whenever we needed it.

Robert said that we must save energy.

Why should I save energy?

Robert knew about energy because he had learned about it at school.

STEAM

BURNING FUEL

"Electricity is energy made by burning fuel – that's coal, oil, and gas," said Robert.

"Cars, trains, and buses
also run on fuel."

15

"Our teacher says the world's fuel supplies won't last forever. If we're not careful, they will run out," said Robert.

"There would be no power for cooking or heating. We'd get cold – and all our food would be cold, too!"

"Buses and trains wouldn't run, so people couldn't get around,

and nothing would reach the stores."

23

"There are many ways to save energy!" said Robert.
"Turn off lights when you don't need them,

close windows and
doors when the
heat is on,

and try putting a sweater
on if you feel cold rather
than the heat."

25

"Going to school by bus or train
uses less fuel than going by car.

You could ride your bike or walk," said Robert.

Robert was right!
Saving energy is easy.
And you might find yourself
doing new
things.

Saving energy saves money too ... so you can have extra treats now and then!

Notes for parents and teachers

Why Should I?

There are four titles about the environment in the *Why Should I?* series: *Why Should I: Save Water? Save Energy? Protect Nature?* and *Recycle?* These books will help young readers to think about simple environmental issues, and other social and moral dilemmas they may come across in everyday life. The books will help children to understand environmental change and how to recognize it in their own surroundings, and also help them to discover how their environment may be improved and sustained. Thinking about saving energy will also teach children to consider others, to act unselfishly, and to share.

Why Should I Save Energy? introduces the subject of energy as a resource and how it can be used either wastefully or wisely. The book introduces a number of simple tasks that children can carry out to help save energy.

Suggestions for reading the book with children

As you read the book with children, you may find it helpful to stop and discuss issues as they come up in the text. Children might like to reread the story, taking on the role of different characters. Which character in the book mirrors their own attitude to energy most closely? How do their own ideas differ from those expressed in the book?

Discussing the subject of energy may introduce children to a number of unfamiliar words, including drafty, energy, environment, fuel, fossil fuels, meter, mining, gasoline, pollution, power station, and precious. Make a list of all the new words and discuss what they mean.

Suggestions for follow-up activities

Discuss the various forms of energy we come across in everyday life. Coal, oil, and natural gas are fossil fuels (so called because they are derived from the fossilized remains of prehistoric plants) that are burned to generate electricity. Most cars and other vehicles run on fuels (gasoline, diesel) made from oil. Batteries store energy. Electricity can also be generated using nuclear power, or by harnessing the energy of sunlight, winds, waves, or running water. These last resources are called renewable resources because, unlike fossil fuels, they will not run out.

Encourage children to make a list of all the things we use energy for, at home, at school, and also in the wider world. Children could inspect electricity or gas meters at home or at school; most meters provide a graphic illustration of how fast energy is being used!

The book suggests a number of things that might happen if local energy supplies ran out. Children might have their own ideas about what could happen and how an energy shortage would affect them. In the wider world, energy is also vital in farming and industry. The book makes a number of suggestions about how energy can be saved. What other ideas can children come up with for saving energy?

Books to read

Amos, Janine. *Pollution.* Orlando, FL: Steck-Vaughn, 1993.
Describes the ways in which our air, water, and soil are being polluted.

Bailey, Donna. *What We Can Do About Conserving Energy.* New York: Franklin Watts, 1992.
Identifies energy conservation issues and gives possible solutions for families and local groups.

Bellamy, David J. *How Green Are You?* New York: Crown Books, 1991.
Provides information and projects about ecology that teach children and their families how to conserve energy, protect wildlife, and reduce pollution.

Berenstain, Stan, and Jan Berenstain. *Berenstain Bears Don't Pollute (Anymore)*. New York: Random House, 1991.
The bears form the Earthsavers Club to teach others how to stop polluting and protect natural resources.

Dorros, Arthur. *Follow the Water from Brook to Ocean.* New York: HarperCollins, 1993.
Follows water from rainfall on the roof to the ocean and explains how important it is to keep our water clean.

Gibbons, Gail. *Recycle! A Handbook for Kids.* New York: Little, Brown & Company, 1996.
Explains the process of recycling from start to finish, focusing on five types of garbage, and describing what happens to each when it is recycled.